Bibliografische Information der Deutschen Nationalbibliothek:
Die Deutsche Nationalbibliothek verzeichnet diese Publikation in
der Deutschen Nationalbibliografie; detaillierte bibliografische
Daten sind im Internet über http://dnb.dnb.de abrufbar.

© 2019 Stephanie Hanel
Herstellung und Verlag:
BoD – Books on Demand, Norderstedt

ISBN: 9783749422555

50 Tage in Brooklyn

50 days in Brooklyn

Stephanie Hanel

edition bilderbusch

Team Tagebuch

Lektorat (dt. Version):
Maren Giering-Desler

Übersetzung ins amerikanische Englisch:
Nick Hanel

Lektorat (engl. Version):
Max Sanderson

Satz und Cover-Gestaltung:
Christine Kern

Zeichnungen:
Stephanie Hanel

Fotos:
Stephanie Hanel, Richard Zinken

Lieben Dank an Euch!

Diary Crew

Copy Editor (German Version):
Maren Giering-Desler

Translation into American English:
Nick Hanel

Copy Editor (English Version):
Max Sanderson

Layout and Cover Design:
Christine Kern

Illustrations:
Stephanie Hanel

Images:
Stephanie Hanel, Richard Zinken

Love to all of you!

Für Ute und Hans

Dedicated to Ute and Hans

Vorab

Mittlerweile befinden wir uns schon im zweiten Jahr unseres New-York-Abenteuers und wie neulich ein netter Amerikaner bemerkte: Das erste Jahr ist das schwierigste, im zweiten fangt ihr an, Euch zu gewöhnen und im dritten wird alles so normal sein, dass ihr Euch nicht mehr vorstellen könnt, woanders zu leben.

Beim Arbeiten an den 50 Tagen habe ich bemerkt, dass sich mein Blick auf die neue Heimat schon deutlich gewandelt hat. Ich habe immer weniger Lust, die Unterschiede zu benennen; merke, dass mir vieles mittlerweile so alltäglich ist, dass ich es nicht mehr diskutieren will. Und wir wechseln sogar in die Verteidigungsrolle, wenn wir zu hören und sehen bekommen, was an verdrehten Berichten über New York in Deutschland als „Nachrichten" verbreitet wird.

Apropos: Was heißt schon „New York"? New Yorker sagen von sich, dass sie in Queens, in Manhattan, der Bronx, Staten Island oder eben Brooklyn leben, also in einem der fünf Boroughs. Brooklyner, die die Art und Weise, wie man dort lebt, lieben, nennen sich gerne Brooklynites. Und Brooklynites untereinander wollen wiederum wissen, in welcher Neighborhood die oder der andere lebt, und haben anhand der Antwort sofort ein Bild vor Augen. Die Neighborhood bestimmt das unmittelbare Lebensgefühl, und wie sagte eine Kollegin aus Deutschland: „Ich glaube, ihr habt ein Bilderbuch-Brooklyn erwischt" – da hat sie Recht.

Ich habe versucht, die 50 Tage so zu lassen, wie sie für uns waren. 50 Tage sind eine willkürliche Einheit, aber so konnte ich unser neues Leben fassbarer machen.

Prologue

Meanwhile we are in the second year of our New York adventure and, as a nice American recently noted, the first year is the hardest; within the second, you'll start to get used to everything; and by the third, things will be so normal, you'll hardly be able to imagine living somewhere else.

During my work on the 50 days I began to recognize that my view towards the new home has begun to change significantly. I am continually losing the will to list out differences, realizing that so much of everyday life has become so ordinary, that I don't feel the need to discuss it any more. We even go into defense mode, if we see or hear any of the twisted reports concerning New York that are published as "news" in Germany.

Come to think of it: what is this "New York", actually? New Yorkers think of themselves as belonging to one of the five boroughs, being Queens, Manhattan, the Bronx, Staten Island, or of course, Brooklyn. Those from Brooklyn who especially love their way of living like to call themselves "Brooklynites". And Brooklynites like to map out their borough by asking fellow Brooklynites which neighborhood they're from. Each neighborhood connotes a specific feeling and situation. As it was recently put by a colleague from Germany: "I think you chose a picture-perfect version of Brooklyn" - she is right.

I tried to keep the 50 days the way they were for us. 50 days is a random unit, but it made our new life easier to grasp. As the dedicated writer you always encouraged me to be, I hope you, Hans, and all the others reading this are able to feel in some ways like you were there with us on our journey. And

Daran möchte ich Dich, lieber Hans, und die anderen, die es zu lesen bekommen, gerne teilhaben lassen. Als engagierte Schreibende, die dazu von Dir immer ermutigt wurde. Und viel Zuspruch von Dir, liebe Ute, bekam. Ich danke Euch von Herzen!

Ein riesengroßes Dankeschön auch an „unsere amerikanische Familie", ohne die es dieses Abenteuer nicht gegeben hätte: Dean und Heidi, Gus, Noah und Max, der zeitgleich in Deutschland ankam und dort Fuß fassen musste, während wir hier auf die Ämter liefen.

Dass Heidi genau wie ich in München geboren wurde und heiratete, kann ich immer noch kaum glauben – was für ein besonderer Zufall!

with all the good wishes and motivation I got from you, Ute, I thank you from the very bottom of my heart!

A huge thanks also goes out to "our American family" without which this adventure wouldn't have existed: Dean, Heidi, Gus, Noah, and Max, who moved to Germany around the time we arrived in New York, and like us was running around from one bureau to the next.

The fact that Heidi was born and married in Munich just as I was, still feels hard to believe – what a special coincidence!

Tag 1

Ab heute mache ich mir wieder Notizen. Bin zu aufgewühlt, um das alles für mich zu behalten.

Paula schickte mir eine Whatsapp, dass sie, um in die Schule zu kommen, alle durch eine Sicherheitskontrolle wie am Flughafen mussten. Erst Taschenkontrolle, dann Metalldetektor. Die Kinder waren mächtig aufgeregt und auch manche Lehrer total überrascht von der Aktion. Es gab wohl eine Mail an die Lehrer, aber die hatten nicht alle gelesen. Falls das ein Dauerzustand werden sollte, will ich nicht mehr, dass Paula hier zur Schule geht.

Heute strahlender Sonnenschein und Richard hatte einen ganz feinen Geburtstagsmorgen.

Bis zu Paulas Nachricht war ich total entspannt, aber nun kommt alles wieder hoch, was seit dem School-Shooting in Florida die Gespräche und Gedanken prägt.

Schöne Überraschung: Elizabeth, eine amerikanische Bekannte, rief mich auf dem Handy an und wir verabredeten uns am Hunde-Strand.

Spaziergang mit Hawk-Watching und Gespräch über interessante Museen und Bücher. Die Unterhaltung schweift aus und plötzlich sagt Elizabeth, dass sie es gar nicht fassen könne, dass Amerika anscheinend nie eine echte Demokratie gewesen und was aus ihrem Land geworden sei.

Day 1

I'm going to start taking notes again. I'm too stirred up to keep all of my thoughts organized properly.

Paula sent me a text saying she had to go through a security check, like the ones at the airport, to enter her school. Bag inspections first, then through a metal detector. The kids and even some of the teachers were shocked. Apparently there had been an email sent to all the teachers, but not everyone had read it. If this should become a regular occurrence, I don't want Paula to go to school here anymore.

Nevertheless, we had beautiful sunshine and Richard had a very pleasant birthday morning.

Until Paula's text reached me, I was totally relaxed, but now I'm thinking about all those conversations and thoughts we've had since the school shooting in Florida.

A nice surprise: Elizabeth, an American acquaintance, called me up and we went to meet at the dog beach.

Our walk included some hawk-watching and chats about interesting museums and books. At a lull in the conversation, Elizabeth said suddenly that she couldn't wrap her head around the apparent fact that America had never been a true democracy.

Tag 2

Sitze schon zum zweiten Mal im Februar draußen im Café „Muse", gleich gegenüber. Welch Luxus!

Richard ist gerade mit sich und dem Job nicht im Reinen und schwer am Grübeln. Es steht viel auf dem Spiel und wir sind als Neulinge hier vielleicht auch leichter verzagt, als wir das sein sollten. Zu Hause musste man sich ja auch ab und zu durchbeißen und konnte nicht das Handtuch werfen. Aber wenn dann Heimweh und sprachlich und kulturell Fremdsein mit in die Waagschale kommen, hängt die so weit runter wie unsere Laune. Müssen wir jetzt wohl durch.

Gerade lief die coole Dogsitterin vorbei. Sie ist sehr athletisch und Paula und ich haben schon gemutmaßt, dass sie Fitness-Trainerin sein könnte ... oder Body-Guard – noch spannender!

Day 2

This is the second time in February I'm sitting outside at Cafe "Muse" across the street. What a luxury!

Richard is under a lot of stress and not yet at peace with his job. There's a lot at stake here, and as "newbies", we're probably more easily discouraged than we should be. At home we also had to fight sometimes, and couldn't just throw the towel in. But here we are weighed down even more by homesickness and the added challenges of a foreign language and culture. Guess we just have to keep at it.

The cool "dogsittress" just passed us. She is very athletic, and Paula and I thought she might be a trainer at the gym... or bodyguard, even more exciting!

Tag 3

Ich – „Harriet the Spy" ;-) – habe herausgefunden, dass bei uns im Viertel die Serie „Dietland" gedreht wird. Eben recherchiert und die interessante Buchvorlage entdeckt: feministische Terroristinnen – wow. Und das soll hier fürs Fernsehen verfilmt werden. Ich staune.

Jetzt schnell zur Metro-Haltestelle, Paula abholen. Unglaublich drückendes Wetter, habe Kreislaufprobleme.

Mittlerweile regnet es, sehr erleichternd, auch wenn wir Sturm- und Flutwarnung aufs Handy bekamen. Mal sehen, wie schlimm es wird. Paula geht morgen jedenfalls nicht in die Schule.

Day 3

I - "Harriet the Spy" ;-) - found out that our block is being used as a set for the show "Dietland". Just did some research and found the interesting book the show is based on: feminist guerrillas - wow. And it's to be broadcasted on local TV. I'm in awe.

Now I'm hurrying to the metro to pick up Paula. Super exhausting weather, feeling drowsy.

Meanwhile it's started raining, which is a relief, although we're now receiving storm and flood warnings on our phones. Let's see how bad it will be. Paula is not going to school tomorrow.

Tag 4

Heute ist mein Buch „Hundert Tage hier – hundert Tage dort" erschienen! Gab auch gleich super nette Reaktionen.

Draußen sturmregnet und schneit es. Egal, was man anzieht, man ist in fünf Minuten pitschnass.

Day 4

Today my book "Hundert Tage hier & hundert Tage dort" (A hundred days here & a hundred days there) was published. Super nice reactions followed immediately.

Heavy snow and rain outside, so whatever you put on, you're soaked within seconds.

Tag 5

Schon mit Lissy im Park gewesen, nett mit Freunden in Deutschland telefoniert und kurz Nick gesprochen. Gleich kommen Thorsten und Isabel und es geht zum Brunchen – kleine Nachgeburtstagsfeier für Richard. Richard kennt Thorsten noch aus seiner Studienzeit. Thorsten arbeitet seit einigen Jahren hier, genau wie Isabel, die Engländerin ist.

Und dann noch ein ausgedehnter Spaziergang im „Prospect Park" zum Bootshaus: just perfect. Das Frühstück im „Piccoli" war dieses Mal sehr familiär, der Kellner super nett und engagiert, das Essen lecker, wir haben viel geteilt – Paula und ich unser gesamtes Mahl – und gelacht.

Best Sunday in quite a while.

Abends noch Fernsehen: Die Oscar-Verleihung war erfrischend selbstironisch und wirkte jünger, spannender, echter. Gefiel uns.

Day 5

Already been to the park with Lissy, had a nice call with friends from Germany and spoke briefly with Nick. Thorsten and Isabel will be around shortly for brunch – we planned a small belated birthday celebration for Richard. Richard has known Thorsten since college. Thorsten has been working here for some years now - so too Isabel, who is originally from England. Finishing things up with a long walk to the boathouse in Prospect Park: just perfect.

Breakfast at Piccoli's was comfortable this time around: family-like atmosphere, waiter super friendly and ambitioned, food delicious, and much to laugh and share – for Paula and me it was the whole meal.

Best Sunday in quite a while.

Some TV to finish off the evening: the Oscar Awards were refreshingly self-ironic and seemed younger, more exciting and more real than ever. We enjoyed them.

Tag 6

Blue Monday. Ständiges Sirenen-Geheul und zwei Hub-schrauber direkt über unserm Haus. Alles, was ich recher-chieren konnte, war ein schwerer Unfall an der großen Kreuzung, auf der ich mich immer wie Freiwild fühle ...

Wie sich später herausstellt, sind ein einjähriges und ein vierjähriges Kind vor den Augen ihrer Mütter überfahren worden. Von einer Frau, die an Multipler Sklerose leidet, ei-nen Anfall hatte und deshalb an der roten Ampel die Kon-trolle über ihr Fahrzeug verlor. Die Mütter und noch ein Passant wurden ebenfalls verletzt.

Day 6

Blue Monday. Constant whining of sirens, and two helicopters have been circling right above the house.

At first the only information I could find was that there had been a big accident at a busy intersection, where I often feel like prey when crossing...

Turns out, two children, ages one and four, were run over by a car, right in front of their mothers, by a woman with multiple sclerosis, who had had a seizure while driving and was unable to stop at the red light. The mothers and another pedestrian were injured as well.

Tag 7

Nun brauche ich mich nicht mehr davor zu fürchten – es ist passiert.

Die neuen Hausbesitzer in Weingarten haben den Kirschbaum gefällt und den Teich zugeschüttet. Ich war überflutet von dem Gefühl, den Baum im Stich gelassen zu haben; schier außer mir bei dem Gedanken an die Frösche; und kann doch nichts tun, als zu akzeptieren, dass das „Paradies" nur noch in der Erinnerung lebt ...

Ich frage mich, warum ich zum Abschied nicht noch einmal in den Baum geklettert bin, und weiß gleichzeitig die Antwort: Dann hätte ich nicht fortgehen können.

Day 7

Now I don't need to be afraid of it anymore - it happened.

The new owners of our house in Weingarten cut down the cherry tree and filled up the pond we built with sand. I was flooded by this feeling that I had somehow abandoned the poor tree; and I was beside myself at the thought of the help-less frogs; but still, I can't do anything, and must accept that this "paradise" has all but vanished from reality, existing now only in memory.

I keep thinking to myself: why didn't I climb the tree one last time? But I know the answer: I wouldn't have been able to leave.

Tag 8

... fing trödelig, in Gedanken versponnen und mit wunderschönen Mails an, die ich gleich zum Morgenkaffee lesen konnte.

Stöckchen-Fieber im Park und prompt bleibt wieder was in Lissys Kiefer stecken. Diesmal bewahre ich die Nerven und bekomme zwar nicht das ganze Stöckchen „herausoperiert", aber kann es zerbrechen. Den einen Teil schluckt Lissy, den anderen spuckt sie aus.

Day 8

... began hesitantly, hazily; head is swimming with thoughts. My morning coffee was accompanied by some beautiful emails.

Lissy was overcome with stick-fever in the park today and promptly got something stuck in her jaw (again). This time I held my nerve and was able to reach the stick and break it in half. Lissy swallowed half and spat out the rest.

Tag 9

Schon wieder konnte ich nicht einschlafen – wie zum Ausgleich wacht Richard immer zu früh auf ... seufz.

Gestern Abend mit Paula im Bett gesessen und den zweiten Teil des niedlichen Eichhörnchen-Zeichentrickfilms angesehen. Das Beste, was man an einem „Immer-noch-Winter"-Abend tun kann.

Heute bin ich auf der Post endlich erfolgreich gewesen und konnte wunderschöne Mond-Briefmarken kaufen.

Am Unfallort waren Kamera-Teams.

Day 9

Couldn't sleep again - Richard still wakes up like he's on German time... sigh.

Sat in bed with Paula last night and watched an adorable animated movie about squirrels. The best remedy for a lingering wintery night.

Today I was finally able to buy the beautiful moon stamps I had noticed earlier at the post office.

Camera teams showed up at the crash site.

Tag 10

Mit Richard auf der Bank gewesen, bekomme nun endlich auch eine Karte für unser amerikanisches Konto.

Bin immer den Tränen nah, wenn ich am Unfallort vorbeikomme. Die Kinderarztpraxis hat eine Hilfsaktion gestartet.

Wenn ich nachts aufwache, denke ich entweder an den gefällten Baum oder die toten Kinder. Was für eine üble Woche.

Richard hadert immer noch mit seinem Job. Ist grad alles ein bisschen viel.

Habe angefangen „Dietland" zu lesen und es war gleich recht gruselig, aber gut geschrieben. Man möchte schon wissen, wie es weitergeht. Und ich kann mir allmählich vorstellen, wie sich das filmisch umsetzen lässt.

Morgen wollen wir uns mit Familie Eimer treffen, hoffentlich klappt das. Sie sind aus Deutschland und leben leider nur für ein Jahr hier.

Day 10

Went to the bank with Richard and finally got a debit card for our American bank account.

I am always close to tears when I go by the crash site. The pediatric clinic started a support program.

When I wake up at night it's either the dead tree or the dead kids on my mind. What a terrible week.

Richard is still struggling with his job. It's all a bit much right now.

Started reading "Dietland" and it comes across as both scary and well written. Really keeps you at the edge of your seat. I imagine it would make for an interesting film.

Tomorrow we planned going to meet the Eimer family, also from Germany, and hopefully it'll work out. Unfortunately, they're only living here for one year.

Tag 11

Schöner Sonntag!

Super nettes Treffen mit Annick, Mischa und ihren Töchtern Emilia und Theresa. Das „New York Transit Museum" hat noch mehr Spaß gemacht als gedacht, weil sie so viele Waggons haben, durch die man laufen darf, weil man Sitze ausprobieren kann und die alten Reklameschilder begutachten und wir uns nebenbei fein unterhielten.

Danach warteten wir zwar ziemlich lange bei „Bareburger", saßen dann aber alle zusammen an einem Tisch. Neue Speisekarte, neue Herausforderung, die ich mit einem dreilagigen Sandwich meisterte.

Kurzer Abstecher zu „Paper Source". Paula und ich fühlten uns richtig heimisch in dem Viertel und dachten wehmütig an unsere „Probewoche" im Juni letzten Jahres zurück. Damals ahnten wir noch nicht, wie sehr sich die Viertel unterscheiden, und dass wir erst nach so vielen Monaten mal wieder in dieser Gegend sein würden. Ich hätte mir nicht vorstellen können, dass sich an dieser einen Straße unsere aufgeregten Erwartungen festhängen würden und uns jetzt als fröhliche Erinnerung wieder zum Lächeln bringen.

Day 11

Nice Sunday!

It was lovely meeting with Annick, Mischa, and their daughters, Emilia and Theresa. The New York Transit Museum made for more fun than we had expected, thanks to the abundance of old train cars, chairs, and advertisement boards on display, which we could freely explore, test out, and observe, in turn. It made a great backdrop to conversation.

After that we waited quite a while to get a table for everyone at Bareburger. The new menu presented an unexpected challenge, but I chose correctly: triple decker sandwich.

Short detour to Paper Source. Paula and I felt very much at home in this particular corner of Brooklyn and wistfully recalled the "trial week" we spent here last June. Back then we didn't realize how much the neighborhoods differed from one another, and also didn't appreciate just how long it would be before we encountered this one again. I hadn't expected our ecstatic first impression of this street to hold true - it brought a smile to our faces.

Tag 12

Ich sehne mich danach, dass es wieder warm genug ist, um auf einer Bank im Park zu sitzen und zu schreiben.

Heute haben sie endlich die Baustelle hier in der Straße „eröffnet", um sich um die marode Gasleitung zu kümmern – was für ein Drama. Wir wollen nicht wissen, was durch die permanenten sinnlosen Feuerwehreinsätze an Geld verschwendet wurde. Und irgendwie wird einem ja auch mulmig, auf Dauer. Man roch Gas in der Straße, aber außer, dass immer wieder mal jemand die Feuerwehr rief, und diese kam, passierte nichts. Vielleicht handelt es noch um einen Frostschaden – hier sind Wasserrohre geplatzt, haben vereiste Fußwege hinterlassen und der Straßenbelag ist gerissen. Unsere Wasserleitung im Haus hatte noch nicht mal eine einfache Schaumstoff-Isolierung, bis der Vermieter eine brachte, weil sie an mehreren Stellen im Haus gefroren war und kein heißes Wasser mehr kam.

In dem speziellen Trödelladen ums Eck gab es heute im Vorbeigehen Spektakuläres zu bewundern. Ein riesiger aus Fundholzstücken zusammengesetzter Hirsch dominiert das eine Fenster. Ein ausgefallenes Gemälde, umrahmt von Seidengewändern und einem Kimono, das andere. Die junge, weiß gekleidete Frau auf dem Gemälde steht zwar klassisch adrett zwischen Blumen, sieht einem aber sehr forsch in die Augen.

Paula hat sich Sushi zum Abendessen gewünscht und Richard hat welches vom Büro aus mitgebracht. Ich bekomme davon leider Brechreiz, aber Paula findet es faszinierend und Richard schmeckt es richtig.

Day 12

I yearn for weather that's warm enough to be able to sit on a bench in the park and write.

Today they finally "opened" the construction site on our street to fix the decrepit old gas pipe - some serious drama going on. We don't want to know how much money has already been wasted on the firefighters' continual, pointless efforts. After a while, the leak tends to make one nauseous. You can often smell the gas from the street, but as long as someone calls the fire department, and they come, nothing happens. Maybe it's all got something to do with frost damage - a number of water pipes have burst, leaving behind icy sidewalks and cracked roads. The water supply in our own house wasn't even properly insulated until the pipes started freezing and the hot water ran out, forcing the landlord to fix the problem.

Today the junk shop around the corner put on quite the spectacular display: a giant stag, made from reclaimed wood, dominated one of the windows; an extraordinary painting, framed by silk-dresses, and a kimono, likewise the second. The young woman in the painting, dressed all in white, stands upright among the loveliest spring flowers, yet her eyes are disturbingly cold and distant, almost lifeless.

Paula asked for sushi for dinner and Richard got some on his way back from the office. Sushi makes me queasy, but Paula finds it fascinating, and Richard really enjoys it.

Tag 13

Die Dreharbeiten zu „Dietland" wurden wegen schlechten Wetters auf Donnerstag verschoben ... Schade, da kann ich gar nicht gucken gehen. War mit Lissy spazieren – der Kimono aus dem Schaufenster ist schon verkauft!

Am wohlsten fühle ich mich, wenn ich so konzentriert auf etwas bin, oder auch so entspannt, dass ich vergesse, wo ich bin. Das soll nicht heißen, dass ich es schrecklich finde, mitten in Brooklyn, sondern meint diese „selbstvergessenen" Momente. Weder übermüdet noch aufgekratzt zu sein, den Körper spüren, aber keine Schmerzen haben, frei, aber nicht ziellos sein, in Bewegung, aber nicht zwanghaft.

Paula hat sich verändert und ich bemerke es auch an mir – kann aber noch nicht beschreiben, was genau es ist.

Day 13

"Dietland" filming was pushed to Thursday due to the bad weather... too bad, I was excited to go and watch. Took Lissy on a walk - the kimono in the junk shop has already been sold!

I feel most comfortable when I am so focused on something, or so relaxed, that I forget where I am. Which isn't to say, that it's somehow horrible, being in Brooklyn: I'm thinking more about those certain moments of flow where I am able to lose myself, where I'm not tired, and not overly-energetic, where I can feel my body, but have no pain, where I feel free, but not aimless, where I can move, but not because I'm forced to.

Paula has changed, and I notice that I have too – but I can't yet describe exactly how.

Tag 14

In Paulas Schule, wie auch landesweit in unzähligen anderen, war heute der Walk-Out in Erinnerung an die Opfer des School-Shootings in Florida und als Zeichen gegen die Macht der Waffen-Lobby.

Der Bürgermeister hatte einen Live-Stream auf Facebook von einer öffentlichen Schule in Brooklyn, den ich unter Tränen angesehen habe. Die Schulsprecher*innen sind alle so mutig – in dem Alter vor laufender Kamera zu sprechen, ist auch für amerikanische Schüler*innen, die ansonsten besser im Auftreten geschult sind, eine große Herausforderung.

Die Schüler*innen-Bewegung ist ein großartiges politisches Hoffnungszeichen. Die Protagonistin Emma Gonzalez und ihre ebenso redegewandten Mitstreiter von der „Parkland-High-School" sind in ihrer Unnachgiebigkeit und gleichzeitigen Erschütterung so beeindruckend, dass sie gerade nicht nur zu Held*innen ihrer Generation werden, sondern auch Erwachsene zutiefst beeindrucken und letztlich beschämen. Die Opfer sind zu Anführer*innen einer Protestbewegung geworden und inspirieren nun Hunderttausende. Nicht die Eltern-Generation, sondern sie selbst verteidigen ihr Leben, ihre Zukunft.

Day 14

Paula's school, along with countless other schools around the country today, participated in a walkout in memory of the victims of the school shooting in Florida and as a protest against the powerful gun lobby.

The mayor's Facebook account posted a livestream from one public school in Brooklyn, which I watched through tears. The students are so brave – speaking in front of a live camera at this age is very difficult, even for American students, who learn more about how to present themselves.

The student movement is a great sign of hope for politics. Its "leader", Emma Gonzalez, and her equally impressive peers from Parkland High School, are so inspiring in the way they hold themselves, despite being visibly traumatized, that they're not just heroes to their own generation: they have outdone many adults. Victims became leaders of a movement, and now they in-  *spire hundreds of thousands of people. They themselves, not their parents, defend their own lives and their own future.*

Tag 15

Heute war ich alleine in Manhattan unterwegs ... Equal Pay Global Forum. Und jetzt bin ich so erschöpft, dass es sofort ins Bett geht.

Aber ganz schnell noch: „Klein-Stephanie" stapfte wacker durch eiskalte Windschneisen von Straßen bis zum riesigen Baustellen-Gelände in Chelsea, zu dem ersten fertigen neuen Wolkenkratzer, in dem sich SAP befindet, fragte sich zur Veranstaltung durch und fuhr mutterseelenallein in einem vollautomatischen Aufzug, der außen fürs entsprechende Stockwerk eingestellt wird und nur dort hält und die Türen öffnet.

Ok, alle Technikfreaks dürfen lachen – ich bin trotzdem stolz auf mich ;-)

Day 15

Today I went to Manhattan on my own... Equal Pay Global Forum. And now I am so exhausted that I will go to bed right away. But quickly:

"Little Stephanie" braved the arctic wind of the open streets all the way to the large construction site in Chelsea, where, in the first new skyscraper on the lot, the new home of SAP, she checked herself into the event and, all alone, rode a fully-automatic elevator, where the level had to be selected before entering, and where the doors opened themselves.

You can laugh at me if you're used to that sort of thing – but I'm still proud of myself ;-).

Tag 16

Food Festival in Paulas Schule!

Wir lernten noch mehr Deutsche kennen, weil es außer meinem einen weiteren Kartoffelsalat gab – sehr lustig. Ist also tatsächlich ein typisch deutsches Essen.

Wenn ich nicht so einen empfindlichen Magen hätte, hätte ich noch viel mehr Speisen kosten wollen – vor allem wäre ich neugierig auf das karibische Essen gewesen ...

Für mich war das Schönste, all die unterschiedlichen Menschen zu sehen und mich so wunderbar mit Paulas Lehrerin Melissa unterhalten zu haben. Ich hätte nicht zu hoffen gewagt, dass das mal so gut klappen könnte und sich so selbstverständlich anfühlt. Sie hat aber auch ein besonderes Talent, auf Menschen zuzugehen.

Alle waren super nett und hilfsbereit, auch das Aufräumen war kein Thema und im Nu gemeinsam geschafft. Unser Heimweg führte uns wieder an den besonders schönen *Brownstones* entlang. Dort in der Dämmerung zu laufen, ist wie in einem romantischen Film spazieren zu gehen.

Day 16

"Food Festival" at Paula's school!

We got to know other Germans, because aside from mine, there was a second potato salad - how funny. It must really be a typical German dish.

If only my stomach wasn't so sensitive, I would have liked to try more dishes - I was especially curious about the Caribbean food ...

The nicest thing for me was meeting all these different people and having a wonderful conversation with Paula's teacher Melissa. I hadn't dared to hope that it would go as well and feel as normal as it did. But she has a special way of going about with people.

Everyone was super nice and helpful, so the cleanup was done in no time. Our way home led us past the especially beautiful Brownstones again. Walking there at dusk is like being in a romantic movie.

Tag 17

Auf dem Hundespaziergang hat mich ein kleines Mädchen niedlich ausgefragt und ihr Opa charmante Kommentare zu meinen Antworten abgegeben. Das war ein Geschenk für ein Kind, zwei Erwachsene und zwei Hunde. Ihrer heißt Sawyer, ist sechs Monate alt und wunderschön grau.

Day 17

On today's "Lissy-walk" a little girl asked me a series of cute questions, and her grandpa commented charmingly on my replies. What a present for a child, two adults and two dogs. Hers, called Sawyer, is six months old and beautifully gray.

Tag 18

... war für mich ein Haushaltstag und für Richard Auskurierzeit. Lissy war nervös, wie immer, wenn Richard krank zuhause ist.

Day 18

...was a housekeeping day for me and a recovery day for Richard. Lissy was nervous, as she always is when Richard is sick at home.

Tag 19

Heute lagen Paula und ich krank in den Betten und Richard ging zur Fahrschule und – yeah! – er hat die Fahrprüfung bestanden!

Das bringt uns allen mehr Freiheit und vor allem sind jetzt die Ostertage in New Jersey gesichert.

Zum feierlichen Abendessen sind wir in die Trattoria „Piccoli" gegangen, wo es wirklich sehr lecker ist. Hatte ganz besondere Ravioli – sie machen die Pasta selbst. Sie ist um Längen besser als die bei „Russo's". Dieses italienische Lädchen in der 7. Avenue steht zwar in einem Brooklyn-Führer, aber wir fanden deren Pasta eher enttäuschend und kaufen da eigentlich nur noch Zwieback oder Panettone.

Day 19

Today Paula and I stayed in our beds, sick, while Richard went to driving school and- yeah! - he passed the driving test!

That provides us with a little more freedom and ensured that we'll be able to drive to New Jersey for Easter break.

We went to the really delicious Trattoria Piccoli for a celebration dinner. I had the ravioli - excellent, and entirely homemade. By far better than what you get at Russo's, a tiny Italian shop on 7th Avenue that we saw in a Brooklyn neighborhood guide. We found their pasta rather disappointing and only ever buy zwieback and panettone there.

Tag 20

Paula hatte schneefrei und wir ließen uns schön einschnei-
en. Lissy war natürlich happy im Park, aber ich ganz schön
fertig danach. Am Spätnachmittag saß ich dann endlich am
Equal-Pay-Artikel – bis in die Nacht.

Day 20

Paula had a snow day and we allowed ourselves to be cheerfully "snowed in". Lissy of course was happy to go to the park, but I was quite finished afterwards. I worked on my equal pay essay from late afternoon on into the night.

Tag 21

Morgen kommt Paulas Freundin Amelie aus Deutschland zu Besuch!

Meine Debit-Card ist endlich freigeschaltet und ich kann mit dem Geld vom Arbeitskonto bezahlen. War sehr aufregend am Bankschalter, da ein einheimisches Dokument zur Legitimation gefragt war. Letztlich klappte es dann mit meiner Arbeitsgenehmigungskarte. Puh!

Lese weiter „Dietland", aber nur in kleineren Happen. Ist eine heftige Lektüre ...

Day 21

Tomorrow Paula's friend Amelie is coming for a visit from Germany!

My debit card is finally activated, so now I can pay with the money in the work account. Was a bit frustrated in the bank because they needed an original document for proof of identity. In the end they accepted my employment card. Phew!

Continuing with "Dietland", but in smaller bites. It's a heavy read...

Tag 22

#Enoughisenough

Das war ein bewegender Triumph der Schüler*innen-Bewegung über die Waffen-Lobby. Wir starrten stundenlang in den Fernseher und es rollten viele Tränen.

Es ist unfassbar, wie viele Menschen in der Menge ihre Hand gehoben haben, als von der Bühne aus gefragt wurde, wer alles schon Familienangehörige durch Waffengewalt verloren hat. Ein junges schwarzes Mädchen sprach für alle schwarzen Frauen und Mädchen, die Opfer von Shootings und noch nicht einmal eine Kurzmeldung wert waren. Eine Überlebende musste sich auf der Bühne übergeben, als sie versuchte, über das Erlebte zu sprechen. Emma schwieg auf der Bühne so lange, wie das Morden des Attentäters in ihrer Schule gedauert hat. Six minutes and 20 seconds – das Schweigen war schier unerträglich.

Day 22

#Enoughisenough

This was a moving triumph of the student movement over the gun lobby. For hours we stared at the TV. Many tears were shed.

It was unbelievable, how many people in the crowd raised their hand when the audience was asked who had lost a family member due to gun violence. A young black girl spoke for all the black women and girls who had been victims of shootings but hadn't gotten any attention. One girl, a survivor, threw up on stage when she tried to describe what she had witnessed. Emma stood silent at the microphone for the same length of time as the attack in her school had taken. Six minutes and 20 seconds - the silence was unbearable.

Tag 23

Häuser mit Parkblick und hinter jeder Türe steht ein Butler, der darauf wartet, sie aufreißen zu dürfen, um die vornehmen Bewohner*innen hinein- oder hinauszulassen: Upper West Side eben.

Das „American Museum of Natural History" war auch dieses Mal spektakulär. Die Dioramen sind bis ins letzte Detail ausgefeilt und sehr aufwändig produziert. Die Diversity-Ausstellung beginnt mit einem Raum, der mich so faszinierte, dass ich erst einmal wie angewurzelt stehen blieb. Dort ist grandios viel zu sehen. Daneben gibt es aber auch hoffnungslos veraltete Abteilungen, die man dann schneller durchschreiten kann. Das war bestimmt nicht mein letzter Besuch dort!

Day 23

Houses with a view of the park and a butler standing behind every door, just waiting to tear it open and make passage for the noble residents: Upper West Side style.

The "American Museum of Natural History" was as spectacular as always. The dioramas are inch-perfect even in the smallest details, so intricately made. The "Diversity Exhibition" began with a room that fascinated me so greatly, I felt like my feet were rooted to the floor. There is an incredible amount to see, discounting a few hopelessly overaged sections - those you can skip over. This was surely not my last visit!

Tag 24

Keine besonderen Vorkommnisse bisher – war mit Amelie im Park und bei „Barnes & Nobles" und jetzt sind Paula und sie zur Bergen Street gefahren und wollen ein bisschen Läden gucken.

Kann's noch gar nicht glauben, dass wir Ostern wirklich ans Meer fahren, so richtig, wie man sich das immer erträumt: in ein weißes Haus direkt am Strand.

Day 24

Nothing special yet – went to the park with Amelie and then to "Barnes & Nobles". Now she and Paula are off to Bergen Street to do some window shopping.

Still can't believe we are going to spend Easter break on the seaside, just the way one always dreams of: in a white house right at the beach.

Tag 25

Heute sind die Mädchen alleine mit der Metro zum „Bryant Park" gefahren und waren später mit Richard am Times Square, den Amelie aus zahlreichen Filmen kannte und sich deshalb sehr wunderte, wie klein das berühmte Areal dann in Wirklichkeit ist.

Sie sahen auch noch im „Hard Rock Café" vorbei – die Sweatshirts und Kappen von dort sind immer noch sehr gefragt.

Wir mussten das Programm insgesamt etwas umstellen, weil das Wetter nicht schön genug ist für „Top of the Rock". „Grand Central" steht auch noch aus. Nach New Jersey gibt es ja noch mehr Sightseeing-Zeit ...

Day 25

Today the girls went to Bryant Park and later with Richard to Times Square, which Amelie knew from countless movies. She was astonished at how small it is in real life.

They also stopped briefly at the Hard Rock Cafe - their sweaters and baseball caps are in high demand.

We had to adjust the program a bit, seeing as the weather wasn't good enough for a visit to the "Top of the Rock". Grand Central is also still on the list. After New Jersey, we'll still have time to go sightseeing...

Tag 26

Bin genervt, weil ausgeblockt durchs Warten auf den Landlord wegen leckender Wasserleitung in der Küche. Als er
dann endlich kommt, höre ich zunächst ein Riesen-Lamento
über die Mieterin, bei der sie zuvor waren, die ihn so furcht-
bar beschimpft und aufgehalten habe. Dann entschied er
nach Besehen des Problems, dass ein neuer Wasserhahn
her muss. Der wurde prompt so lustig montiert, dass wir
jetzt warmes Wasser bekommen, wenn man denkt, es käme
kaltes, und umgekehrt. Außerdem lässt der Hahn sich nicht
mehr übers ganze Waschbecken schwenken. Aber wir wollen
nicht undankbar sein: Immerhin läuft nirgends mehr Wasser, wohin es nicht soll.

Day 26

I'm annoyed from having to wait for the landlord, because the kitchen water pipe decided to start leaking. When he finally arrived, I got to listen to a long complaint about the last tenant he saw, who was apparently horribly rude and held him up. He then decided, after examining the problem, that we needed a new tap. It was then installed so laughably, that now warm water comes out, when you expect cold, and vice versa. Furthermore, the tap itself can no longer be moved across the full range of the sink. But we don't want to be ungrateful: at least there is no more water running where it's not supposed to.

Tag 27

Trallala – wie immer gehofft, es könnte unaufwendiger sein, eine kleine Reise zu machen. Eine super aufgeregte Tochter gab's obendrauf ... aber nun sind wir alle am Meer und die Nerven können sich beruhigen. Endlich Auslauf und Platz für alle!

Das Häuschen ist geschmackvoll eingerichtet und sehr gemütlich. Besser hätten wir es nicht erwischen können. Richard hat eben lecker gekocht und jetzt sind alle außer mir zum Strand hinunter, den Sonnenuntergang ansehen. Ich brauchte es gerade kuschelig und ruhig.

Der Einkaufsausflug mit Richard vorher war speziell. Wir sind ja jetzt auf dem Land, also: wilde Typen im Alkohol-Laden, die Verkäuferin sieht nach Bar-Dame aus, und als wir mit lautem Brummen die Protzkiste starten, die Richard bei AVIS bekommen hat, gibt es zustimmendes Grinsen. Das große Auto-Los zog Richard, weil das bestellte Auto nicht da war und es zur Entschädigung ein Upgrade gab.

Ansonsten waren wir noch in einem Naturkostladen, der alles geschlagen hat, was wir bis dahin gesehen hatten, und auf einem Sprung bei Aldi. Tolle Kombi also ...

Und nun sind wir tatsächlich in „unserem" blau-weißen Haus, haben einen Wintergarten, einen Balkon, eine Terrasse im Sand und von überall direkten Blick in die Ferne ohne ein einziges Hindernis!

Mittlerweile liegt Lissy schnarchend zwischen Sofa und Sessel und die Mädchen sind in ihrem Zimmer. Man hört ein

Day 27

As always, we hoped it would be less effort to go on a little trip - not so. A super hectic daughter to boot... but now we've arrived at the sea and nerves can settle. Finally some space for us all!

The house is styled with good taste, and very comfy. We couldn't have chosen better. Richard made some delicious food and now everyone is off to the beach to watch the sunset - except for me. Right now, I need quiet and comfort.

The shopping trip with Richard before was something else. We're in the countryside now, of course, and: wild-looking guys in the liquor store, woman at the counter looked like a real barkeeper, and when we revved up the fancy car that Richard got at Avis, we were met with approving grins. Richard chose this one after it turned that the car we or-

wenig die Brandung ... und eben glühten die letzten Sonnenstrahlen. Nun wird es richtig Nacht.

Ich lese noch, Richard schläft, die Mädchen sind auch in den Betten, aber noch munter am Reden, so gehört das ja auch ...

dered was unavailable and they gave us a free upgrade to compensate.

Other than that we went by an organic market that beat everything we had seen up to that point, and also stopped briefly at Aldi. Certainly an interesting combo...

And now we really are at "our" blue-white beach house, and have a winter garden, a balcony, a terrace in the sand and a clear view of our surroundings, without any obstacles in any direction!

Lissy is already sprawled out in the space between the couch and the armchair, snoring, and the girls are in their room. There's the gentle surge of the ocean... and the glow of the day's final rays of sunlight. Now it's turning into night.

I'm reading, still, while Richard is sleeping. The girls are in their beds, but still chatting away... just like it's supposed to be...

Tag 28

Beim Mittagessen ein bisschen „Amerika-auf-dem-Land"-
Eindrücke gesammelt, neugierig in die Gegend geguckt, etwas Berührungsängste abgebaut und Spaß mit unserem
peinlichen Auto gehabt.

Day 28

At lunch we gained some "American countryside experience" curiously observing neighborhood and people. Had some fun with our embarrassing car.

Tag 29

... ganz früh am Morgen einen Weißkopfseeadler am Strand gesichtet!

Richard hatte mich um fünf Uhr unabsichtlich geweckt. Wir haben lecker Milchkaffee getrunken und ein erstes getoastetes Croissant gegessen und dann wurde es auch langsam hell.

Später suchten wir uns einen Horseshoe-Crab-Panzer als Andenken.

Viel „Frohe Ostern" gewünscht, per Telefon und Whatsapp.

Ostereier-Suche rund ums Haus, aber leider nicht im Sand, wegen Lissy. Sie hat es aber trotzdem – wie jedes Jahr – geschafft, sich zumindest ein kleines Schoko-Ei zu schnappen. Für die Hundefreund*innen: Ja, wir wissen, dass Hunde keine Schokolade fressen sollen.

Jetzt bereiten Paula und Richard Lasagne vor und Lissy schläft geduscht hinter dem Sessel.

Nachmittags wurde es überraschend noch mal sonnig, die Mädels waren lange am Strand und haben später Muscheln gefärbt. Richard und ich saßen mit Lissy zusammen auf der Terrasse in den Holzstühlen und sahen in die Dünen. Ab und zu fiel uns etwas ein, das wir uns mitteilten, dann wieder saßen wir lächelnd da und freuten uns über unseren glücklichen Hund, lauschten auf das Lachen der Mädchen, waren einfach nur da und hätten gerne die Zeit angehalten.

Day 29

...saw a bald eagle early this morning at the beach!

Richard woke me up unintentionally at five in the morning. We had delicious cappuccino and our first toasted croissants and then it slowly turned bright.

Later we sought out a horseshoe crab shell as a keepsake.

Wished many "Happy Easters" with calls and WhatsApp's.

Egg hunt around the house, but sadly nothing hidden in the sand, because of Lissy. But still she managed - as she does every year - to find herself at least one chocolate egg. For any

dog lovers reading this: yes, we know dogs aren't supposed to eat chocolate!

Now Paula and Richard are making lasagna and Lissy, freshly bathed, is sleeping behind the armchair.

In the afternoon it suddenly became sunny again, so the girls were at the beach for a long time and afterwards colored some shells together. Richard and I sat on the terrace with Lissy watching the dunes. From time to time we thought of things to say, but mostly, we just sat there smiling, glad that the dog was content, and listened to the girls' laughter, wishing we could stop time forever.

Tag 30

Packen hat gut geklappt und die Fahrt war unspektakulär. Aber der Abschied vom Häuschen fiel so schwer, dass wir beschlossen wiederzukommen.

Wir werden nun doch noch mal zur Tierarztpraxis gehen, da Lissy ständig hechelt – wir warten nur gerade ab, ob uns eine mit Richards Eltern befreundete Tierärztin einen Rat geben kann, auf was wir sie am besten untersuchen lassen sollten ... Auf alle Fälle hatte sie eine wunderschöne Zeit am Meer.

Day 30

Packing went well and the drive back was unspectacular. Saying goodbye to the house was so difficult, that we had to promise ourselves we would return again sometime.

We're going to the vet now, because Lissy keeps panting. Just waiting on a friend of ours in Germany, also a vet, to get back to us: we asked her if there's anything we should have specifically looked at... in any event, Lissy had a beautiful time at the sea.

Tag 31

Auf dem Hundespaziergang im Little-Library-Kasten ein Buch erspäht, das ich eh schon immer mal lesen wollte: „Daddy-Long-Legs" von Jean Webster. Das Cover gefällt mir zwar nicht besonders, aber trotzdem hatte ich das Gefühl, dieses Büchlein könnte den Tag retten. So war es dann auch! Schon ein Buch in der Hand zu tragen, half ein wenig, die Kälte und Nässe zu vergessen, die so gar nicht frühlingshaft ist.

Das Buch ist sehr anrührend, auch wenn mir der Plot nicht gefällt – es ist schon etwas Besonderes. Die arme Autorin starb mit 39 bei der Geburt ihrer Tochter. Ihr Buch ist ein Schatz! Der auch heute noch immer wieder aufs Neue gehoben wird, wie man an mir sehen kann. Erstveröffentlichung 1912 ...

Day 31

While out walking the dog, I came across a book I had always wanted to read in one of those "Little Library Boxes": Daddy-Long-Legs, by Jean Webster. I don't really like the cover, but still, I had the feeling that this little book might make my day. And it did! Just the feeling of having a book in my hand helped me forget about all this cold, wet weather, which is so not spring-like.

The book is very touching, and even though I don't particularly like the plot, it is still something special. The poor author died at the age of 39 while giving birth to her daughter. Her book is a treasure! Published originally in 1912... how amazing, that even today, it can be unearthed and read, as in my case.

Tag 32

Heute war ich mit Amelie und Paula erst Pizza essen und dann im „Transit Museum". Direkt vor den Fenstern des Pizza-Lokals geht es hinunter zur Metro, also ein perfekter Platz zum Gucken. Was wir ausgiebig taten.

Das „Transit Museum" hat ebenfalls einen Metro-Abgang, da es sich in einer ehemaligen Station befindet. Die Werbung in den alten Waggons fasziniert mich immer wieder – da könnte man soziologische Studien anstellen: Frauenbild, Anstand/Moral, Thema „Heimatfront", Gesundheit, Schönheitsideale, alles da! Da gibt es eine „Miss Subway"-Wahl, bei der man von den Kandidatinnen erfährt, was sie für eine Ausbildung und was für Lebensträume sie haben, da wird in Comics dazu aufgerufen, sich im sozialen Miteinander in der Bahn und auf der Straße fair und höflich zu verhalten, da werden Seifen und Kaugummi angepriesen, da springt eine Badenixe im pinken Kostüm tollkühn in die Fluten und eine Dame schlägt einen Herrn beim Tennis, der entsprechend ver-

grämt aussieht. Eine Anzeige wirbt für die „Campfire Girls" – zu Hause lese ich nach: Wie schon vermutet, war das eine Pfadfinderinnen-Vereinigung.

Day 32

Today Amelie, Paula and I went out for pizza before visiting the Transit Museum. The pizza place has windows right in front of the subway entrance - a perfect place to observe passersby. Which we did.

The Transit Museum also has such an entrance, since it's actually located inside a former station. The ads in the old train cars fascinates me again and again - they could be topics for sociological experiments: perceived images of women, virtue and morality, inside the home front, health, symbols of beauty, and so on. It's all there! There's a "Miss Subway" con-

test showing information about different candidates: what their education was, what their dreams were; there are comics calling for people to behave politely in public transportation; there is soap and chewing gum on display; there is a mermaid in a pink costume, jumping recklessly into high tides; and a man is being beaten by a lady at tennis, and looking accordingly grumpy. One ad campaign for the "Campfire Girls" - did some research at home, and as assumed, it was for girl scouts.

Tag 33

Eigentlich wollten Amelie, Paula und ich eine romantische Staten-Island-Ferry-Tour machen, aber dank österlichem Touristenandrang war es eher eine soziale Herausforderung. Immerhin haben wir die Statue of Liberty gesehen und wieder einen Punkt auf der Besichtigungsliste abhaken können.

Anschließend nutzten wir Richards Mittagspause, gingen alle zusammen in ein nahegelegenes Irish Pub und waren sehr zufrieden mit unserem Essen.

Abendlicher Aufbruch zum „Rockefeller Center", wo ich Blumen und überdimensionale Ostereier bewundern konnte, während die Mädchen die Läden inspizierten. Richard kam nach und wir stellten uns in die Schlange für „Top of the Rock" an, um wenig später zu erfahren, dass es für heute keine Eintrittskarten mehr geben würde.

Spontane Planänderung und Taxifahrt zum High-Line-Einstieg in Chelsea, wo wir einen wunderbaren, allerdings auch bitterkalten, Sonnenuntergangs-Abendspaziergang machten. Die High-Line-Umgebung ändert sich rasant – konnte man am Anfang noch auf kleinere, kreativ bewohnte Häuserblocks gucken, glänzt jetzt eine glatte Fassade neben der nächsten. Trotzdem ist das „Zwischen-den-Häusern-Schweben" immer noch ein spezielles Erlebnis. Abstecher in den „Chelsea Market", den ich gar nicht so besonders fand und mir viel mehr wie einen echten Markt und nicht wie eine überdachte Fress-Mall vorgestellt hatte, und dann ab mit dem Uber nach Hause und aufwärmen.

Day 33

Amelie, Paula and I had wanted to go on one of those romantic Staten Island Ferry tours, but thanks to the tourist rush around Easter time, it became too much of a hassle. Still, we saw the Statue of Liberty close and were able to check off another box on the sightseeing list.

Afterwards, we used Richard's lunch break to get some food at a nearby Irish pub, which was very satisfying.

In the evening we went to Rockefeller Center, where I admired the flowers and oversized Easter egg decorations while the girls checked out the shops. Richard followed later and we got in the line for the "Top of the Rock", only to be told moments later that ticket sales were finished for the day.

Spontaneous change of plans: we took a taxi to the entrance for the High Line in Chelsea, where we had a wonderful, but also freezing cold, sunset walk. The view from the High Line is rapidly changing - you used to see smaller, creatively inhabited housing complexes, now it's just one smooth facade after the next. Even so, the "hovering in between buildings" feeling you get on the walk is still quite special. We visited Chelsea Market, but I was disappointed to find out that it wasn't a "real market" as I had imagined, and more of a food court with a roof. After that we took an Uber home and warmed ourselves up.

Tag 34

Geburtstag.

Ursprünglich sollte es in den Botanischen Garten gehen, aber dafür war das Wetter zu schlecht, deshalb wünschte ich mir, dass wir uns das „Skizzenbuch-Museum" in Williamsburg ansehen.

Dort angekommen, begrüßte uns eine junge Frau und machte uns mit der Bibliotheks-Ordnung vertraut: Man darf die Skizzenbücher leider, aber verständlicherweise, nicht selbst aus dem Regal ziehen, sondern kann an einem Tablet recherchieren und sich welche geben lassen. Doch es gibt einen großen Tisch und alle Büchlein, die dort in einem Drahtkorb liegen, sind frei zugänglich.

Gleich die ersten, die ich in die Hand nahm, waren sehr spannend – bei zweien wurde ich richtig ehrfürchtig und

Day 34

My birthday.

Originally I had wanted to go to the Botanical Garden, but the weather was poor, so I chose to visit the "Sketchbook Project" exhibition in Williamsburg instead.

We were welcomed there by a young woman who told us the museum rules: sadly, but understandably, you're not allowed to take the sketchbooks from the shelves on your own; you have to check them out on a tablet before they are brought to you. Still, there's a large table with a bunch of little books in a wire basket, and these were all free to access.

The first ones I grabbed were immediately very exciting. I was totally awestruck by two of these, and one of them was just plain fun. They were made by Swedish, South Korean and American women, respectfully. At the end of our visit, Richard got me an "official" sketchbook, meaning: I can participate in the project myself, and have something to leave behind in New York.

Back at home we had Paula's specialty, which she prepared with Amelie: a desert with several layers of cake-dough, yogurt, berries and oranges, served in a glass.

eins hat einfach Spaß gemacht. Sie sind von einer Schwedin, einer Süd-Koreanerin und einer Amerikanerin gestaltet worden. Zum Abschied bekam ich von Richard auch so ein „heiliges" Skizzenbuch geschenkt und kann mich nun am Projekt beteiligen und etwas in New York hinterlassen.

Zu Hause gab es Paulas Spezialität, die sie mit Amelie zusammen vorbereitet hatte: eine Nachspeise mit verschiedenen Schichten aus Kuchenteig, Joghurt, Beeren und Orange im Gläschen.

Zum Abendessen hatte ich mir das „Hooked" gewünscht, dass ich jeden Tag beim Hundespaziergang sehe, in dem wir aber noch nie waren. Freudig aufgekratzt unterhielten wir uns auf Paulas Fragen hin über Traumorte, Wunschträume und Lebensorte überhaupt. Auch über Heimat. Das Essen schmeckte hervorragend, allerdings hatte Amelie zwei Burgerbrötchen-Unterseiten und Paula zwei Oberseiten … woran der Koch wohl gedacht hat? Unsere Gedanken flogen jedenfalls hoch und heiter: von Paulas Staubkorn-Idee über Amelies niesende Taube bis zu meinem Eichhörnchen auf dem Dach – im Nu entstand eine Kinderbuchserie. Beschwingter Heimweg.

For dinner I wanted to go to the "Hooked" restaurant, where we hadn't been yet, even though Lissy and I pass by it on a daily basis. Happily animated, we discussed Paula's questions about dream destinations, aspirations and in general places to live. Also, what "home" is. The food was delicious, but Amelie received two bottom buns with her burger and Paula two top buns... had the cook been distracted by something? Our ideas were all over the place: Paula's dust particle theory, the sneezing pigeons of Amelie or my own squirrels on the rooftop. And just like that, we had a series of children's books plotted out. Cheerful walk home.

Tag 35

Amelie und Paula fuhren noch mal nach Manhattan. Richard, Lissy und ich trabten zur Tierarztpraxis „Animal Kind".

Der Wartebereich füllte sich rasch und ich kam aus dem Gucken, welche Vierbeiner mit welchen Besitzer*innen auflaufen, gar nicht mehr raus: stolzer Windhund-Besitzer, selbstredend distinguiert, quirliges Hündchen mit einem stämmigen jungen Pärchen, Familie mit kleinem Jungen und einem Welpen, Mann mit Bulldogge, älteres Ehepaar mit überschlankem Labrador und zwei Männer mit einem hyperventilierenden Mops.

Wir kamen gerade rechtzeitig dran, um einer Frau mit Hund im Tragetuch Platz zu machen, und diesmal begrüßte uns eine jüngere, aber souverän wirkende Tierärztin. Sie tippt wegen Nasen- und Augenproblemen auf Allergie, verschreibt aber wegen der aktuellen Entzündungen Augentropfen und Antibiotika.

Kurze Aufregung, weil die Subway wegen Reparaturarbeiten die Station, an der die Mädchen aussteigen wollten, übersprungen hat, aber dank Handy-Anweisungen landen sie wieder gut zu Hause.

Zum Schluss eines Besuchs scheint die Zeit immer schneller zu laufen, jedenfalls schnurren die Stunden zusammen und es ist Zeit für die Abfahrt. Paula und Richard bringen Amelie mit dem Uber zum Flughafen und ich sehe mich erstaunt in der leeren Wohnung um.

Day 35

Amelie and Paula went to Manhattan again. Richard, Lissy and I walked to the vet place, "Animal Kind".

The waiting room was quickly filled up and I couldn't keep track of which four-legged friend belonged to which human: a greyhound and its proud owner stood out, certainly; a small, feisty dog with a heavyset young couple; a family with a small boy and a puppy; man with a bulldog; elderly couple with a very skinny lab; and two men with a hyperventilating pug.

When our turn came, we made space in the waiting room for a woman with her dog in a baby sling. A young, confident seeming woman greeted us this time. She guessed that Lissy might be having allergy problems, based on issues she seemed to be having with her eyes and nose, but prescribed eye drops and an antibiotic for the current infection.

Quick moment of chaos when the girls' subway skipped the station they had wanted to get out at, due to ongoing repairs, but thanks to instructions from Richard they found their way back home safely.

Towards the end of a visit, time always seems to run faster. Somehow, it's already time to say goodbye. Paula and Richard went to take Amelie to the airport in an Uber and now I find myself gazing confusedly around an empty apartment.

Tag 36

Paula soll mit einem Familienmitglied ein Interview zum The- ma „Coming of Age" machen und heute haben wir uns dafür zusammengesetzt. Sie hat geschickt nachgefragt, mich er- muntert, oder hilfreiche Sätze eingestreut. Finde ich klas- se, dass sie so etwas in der Schule lernt – neulich waren sie auch am „Grand Central" und mussten Passanten befragen. Diese Woche werden sie zu einer Bibliothek fahren und dort weiter an dem Interview arbeiten – also ganz so, wie es hier viele Journalist*innen machen. Musste ich gleich an Annick und Mischa denken. Das Lernen ist hier überhaupt viel mehr mit praktischen Dingen verknüpft und wirkt auf mich wie eine Einführung in Studien-Methoden und das Erwachse- nen-Arbeitsleben. Eine tolle Chance für alle, die sich schwer tun mit reiner Wissensaufnahme. Ich will da gar nicht das eine gegen das andere aufwiegen, bin nur angetan, wie gut Paulas Talente hier zur Entfaltung kommen.

Day 36

Paula is supposed to hold an interview with a family member about the topic "Coming of Age" and today we sat down together to do just that. She asked smart questions, and encouraged me, throwing in lots of helpful sentences. I think it's great, that she learns stuff like this in school – recently she was even at Grand Central and had to ask questions to pedestrians. This week they'll go to a library to work on their interviews – just as many journalists here do. It reminded me of Annick and Mischa. Learning in general is far more connected to practical things here and seems to serve as more of an introduction into different methods of study and adult work life, which is great for all those who have trouble with more traditional, information-based learning. I'm not trying to compare one to the other, I am just fascinated by how Paula's talents have blossomed here.

Tag 37

Das war nicht nur der längste Sommer meines Lebens, letztes Jahr, sondern ist nun auch der längste Winter – heute ist der 9. April und wir haben weiterhin 2 Grad.

Lissy hat mich im Park völlig aus der Fassung gebracht, weil sie nicht davon abzubringen war, einen abartig spitzen Knochen zu verschlingen, den sie aus einem Laubhaufen erschnüffelt hatte. Grässlich. Nie wieder ein Labrador! Ich bin diesen ewigen Kampf und die Sorge und das Rechtfertigen so leid: Futter. Futter. Futter. Herrje.

Heute die Anmeldung meines Skizzenbuchs abgeschlossen – morgen soll es losgehen. Habe ja Zeitdruck: Ende April ist die vorgegebene Abgabefrist aller Skizzenbücher aus diesem Schwung.

Day 37

Not only did I experience, in the last year, the longest-lasting summer of my life, but apparently also the longest-lasting winter – today is April 9th and it's still barely above freezing.

Lissy made me furious at the park today. She sniffed out an unusually spiky bone from a pile of leaves and I couldn't get it out of her mouth. Gross. Never again, a lab! I am so sick of this constant fight, the worries about her health, and justifying her eating habits. Food. Food. And more food. My goodness.

Today I officially registered my sketchbook for the exhibition – I'll start working on it tomorrow. Under a bit of pressure, though: the deadline to hand it in is at the end of April.

Tag 38

Heute Nacht wollte ich im Dunkeln auf die Toilette und wunderte mich, dass ich plötzlich etwas Hartes unter meinem Hausschuh hatte. Als mir einfiel, was es sein könnte, schaltete ich schnell das Licht ein: Tatsächlich – erbrochene Stücke von dem spitzen Knochen!

Tagsüber fünf Blätter vom Skizzenbuch gefüllt – nun bin ich optimistisch, dass es klappen kann.

Abends kam Richard früher heim, weil ich uns Karten für die Vorstellung von Madeleine Albrights neuem Buch besorgt hatte. So machten wir uns zu Fuß auf den Weg, bewunderten die Magnolienbäume vor den Brownstones und kamen erwartungsvoll bei der „Congregation Beth Elohim"-Synagoge an. Die Eintrittskarten konnte man vor Ort in „Facism – A Warning" umtauschen – es war Erstveröffentlichungstag.

Vor dem Veranstaltungsgebäude standen ein paar Polizisten und beim Gang zur Toilette entdeckte ich, dass sie sich auch den Keller ansahen, aber insgesamt wirkte alles entspannter als erwartet. Frau Albright betritt die Bühne nahezu leichtfüßig. Achtzig ist eine Zahl, die man schier nicht in Verbindung bringen kann mit dieser Frau, die uns da von der Bühne herab in den Blick nimmt.

Albright spricht glasklar und hat eine angenehm zurückgenommene Stimme. Nichts bringt sie aus der Fassung – auch nicht die drei aufeinanderfolgenden Protestaktionen von drei sehr aufgebrachten Menschen, die ihr vorwerfen, für den Tod einer halben Million Kinder verantwortlich zu sein (wegen der Sanktionen gegen den Irak). Es gelingt, die Pro-

Day 38

Last night I went to the bathroom in the dark and stepped on some kind of hard object. As I reached to turn on the light, I already had a suspicion of what it might be - and just as I guessed, pieces of the spiky bone!

Over the day I filled five pages of the sketchbook and now I'm feeling optimistic that I'll have it done in time.

In the evening Richard returned home a bit earlier than usual. I got us tickets for the release of Madeleine Albright's new book. So we headed off on foot, admiring the magnolia trees in front of the Brownstones along the way, and arrived full of expectations at the "Congregation Beth Elohim" synagogue, where the event took place. The tickets could be swapped for "Fascism – A Warning" at the door, since it was the day of release.

testierenden ohne Polizei nach draußen zu geleiten, die Rabbinerin mahnt zum vernünftigen Umgang miteinander und dann kann die Veranstaltung fortgesetzt werden. Nachdem es vor den geschlossenen Türen aber noch länger ziemlich lautstarke Parolen gab, hat die Polizei vor Ort wohl Verstärkung geordert – jedenfalls hört man bald Sirenen näherkommen. Dann herrscht Ruhe.

They placed some cops in front of the building and on my way to the restroom I discovered they were also watching over the basement, but overall everything seemed more relaxed than expected. Mrs. Albright is almost fleet-footed going on stage. Eighty is a number you can barely bring into connection with this lady, who confidently takes us in from the stage.

Albright speaks crystal-clear and has a comfortably gentle voice. Nothing flusters her – not even three consecutive protest actions, by three very furious people, accusing her of being responsible for the death of half a million children (because of the sanctions against Iraq). They manage to escort the protestors outside without the police's help. The female rabbi speaks briefly about interacting responsibly with each other and then the program continues. Because you could still hear loud chants from behind the closed doors, the police had to call for reinforcements. You could hear the sirens approaching. Then it was silent.

Tag 39

Zum ersten Mal frühlingshafter Hundespaziergang! Wie schön, über freie Wiesen zu schreiten. Alle Zäune sind abmontiert, sogar der um die besondere Baumgruppe. Gefühl von Freiheit und Größe – „mein" Park.

Mittlerweile habe ich im Netz gesehen, dass zu einem Protestmarsch sowohl zu dem Buchladen, der zur Veranstaltung eingeladen hatte, als auch zu der Veranstaltung selbst aufgerufen worden war. Allerdings von Aktivisten, die mit krassen Bildern und unzulässigen Verteufelungen agieren. Tatsächlich werfen sie Albright vor, eine Kriegshetzerin zu sein – mit dem im Zusammenhang mit ihrem Buch kolportierten „call to arms" ist aber ziviler Ungehorsam gemeint. Der Stuhl, von dem aus die Demokratie verteidigt werden müsse, sei in den USA unbesetzt, sagte sie. Albright war eine Hardlinerin und sie hat sich auch nicht zur Philosophin gewandelt, aber gestern Abend sprach eine Realpolitikerin über Erfahrungen, die ihr der Lebensweg mitgegeben hat, eine gebildete Frau über politische Systeme und eine Weltreisende über die Entwicklung führender Männer, die sie von früher persönlich kennt und die sich nun, an der Macht, als Unterdrücker der Freiheit entpuppen.

Paula kam heute mit so vielen verschiedenen Themen von ihrem Schulausflug heim, dass ich etwas überfordert war. Auf alle Fälle haben sie im Museum auch einen guten Film über den englischen Naturforscher Henry Walter Bates gezeigt bekommen: „Amazon Adventures". Leider kann man den nur als Lehrfilm und nicht im Kino sehen.

Day 39

First spring-like dog walk! How beautiful it was wandering over the uncovered meadows. All the fences are down, even those around the "special tree section". Had the feeling of freedom and space – "my" park.

By now I discovered online that they called for a protest march to the bookstore that hosted the event, in addition to the one at the event itself. The activists are provoking with extreme images and undue slander, though. They're accusing Albright of being a warmonger – but the actual meaning of the "call to arms" associated with her book was civil disobedience. The chair from which democracy needs to be defended is unoccupied in the US, she says. Albright used to be a hardliner, and she hasn't exactly become a philosopher, but last night we heard a political realist, a Realpolitikerin, speaking on her life's experiences; an educated woman speaking on political systems; a world traveler speaking on the powerful men she knows from past years, who, now that they are in power, have revealed themselves to be suppressors of freedom.

Paula slightly overwhelmed me with all the different topics she returned with from her field trip today. In any case they got to see a good movie about the English natural scientist Henry Walter Bates at the museum: "Amazon Adventures". Sadly you can only watch it as an educational movie, and not in theaters.

Tag 40

Letzte Nacht von allen möglichen Leuten aus Weingarten
geträumt. Sogar Herr Breitenstein war wieder lebendig
und strahlte mit seinen kugelrunden Augen aus dem ver-
schmitzt-zerknitterten Gesicht. Es tut mir immer noch leid,
dass wir auf Reisen waren, als er starb, und deshalb auch
nicht zur Beerdigung gehen konnten. Und noch mehr, dass
ich nie Fotos von ihm gemacht habe, weil ich es mir von ihm
ausreden ließ. Aber meine Erinnerung im Traum und auch
jetzt zeichnet ein ganz klares Bild.

Hm, scheint eine neue Melancholie-Welle zu rollen ...

Day 40

Last night I dreamed of everybody back in Weingarten. Even Herr Breitenstein was alive again, smiling brightly, roly-poly eyes shining from his mischievous, wrinkled face. I still regret that we were traveling when he passed away and had to miss the funeral. And I regret that I allowed myself to be convinced by him, never to take his picture. At least the memories from my dreams, and the ones I have now, paint a detailed picture.

Hm, apparently there is a new wave of melancholy rolling in...

Tag 41

Für die politische Niedergeschlagenheit gibt es übrigens einen Namen, meinte neulich eine Bekannte: Trump-Depression. Gerade lässt er Syrien bombardieren. Ich brauche heute dringend Trost. Mal sehen, ob das Zeichnen im Skizzenbuch hilft.

Der Spaziergang mit Lissy brachte wieder einen Hauch Frühling!

Als ich heimkam, gab es kein Wasser mehr aus der Leitung – schon zum zweiten Mal. Immer noch Baustellen rund um unser Haus, wegen des Gasproblems. Wenn Wasser abgesperrt wird, muss das offensichtlich nicht groß angekündigt werden ... Kurzerhand beschloss ich, ins „Muse" zu gehen und dort Mittag zu essen. Paula, die Kopfgrippe hat, gleich mit an die frische Luft genommen. So saßen wir dann im Halbschatten draußen und verspeisten unsere Omeletts.

Morgen treffen wir Karen, eine Freundin von Richard aus Deutschland, und ihre Tochter Sarah, die sich einen gemeinsamen Ausflug nach New York gönnen. Sarah habe ich zuletzt als kleines Mädchen auf unserer Hochzeit gesehen und nun studiert sie!

Day 41

As an acquaintance recently taught me, there is a name for the current political dejection: Trump-Depression. Just now he commanded further bombings on Syria. I really need something comforting today. Let's see if drawing in the sketchbook will help.

The walk with Lissy hinted of spring!

When I got home there was no water from the tap – second time now. There are still construction sites surrounding our house because of gas leaks. Apparently they don't have to announce upfront that they are going to cut off water...

Spontaneously decided to go to Muse for lunch. Paula, who has the flu, came along to get some fresh air. So we found ourselves sitting together in the semi-shade outside the diner eating omelets.

Tomorrow we are going to meet Karen, a friend of Richard's from Germany, accompanied by her daughter, who decided to go on a trip to New York. The last time I saw Sarah was at our wedding, when she was a little girl - and now she studies!

Tag 42

Um acht Uhr ging es los mit unserem Besuch in Richtung Park, zum großen Hunde-Freilauf. Auf dem Weg mussten wir ab und an pausieren, weil Lissy so schnaufte, aber alle waren bester Laune. Lissy trabte sogar von sich aus zu fremden Hunden und schnüffelte hier und da, die Sonne schien, viele Hundebesitzer*innen hatten den Coffee to go schon in der Hand und plauderten angeregt mit Freunden und Bekannten – wir stoppten auf dem Heimweg beim bewährten Café „Muse" und frühstückten an der gemütlichen Eckbank, unter der sich auch für Lissy ein Platz fand. Es ist schon warm genug, um draußen zu sitzen, aber die Luft ist noch klar.

Später ging es zum „Brooklyn Bridge Park" und nach einem schönen Spaziergang verabschiedeten wir die Besucherinnen auf die Fähre zur Wall Street – besser als Metro fahren. Wir konnten alle noch lange winken. Auf der Heimfahrt zum Taxifenster hinausgespäht: überall blühende Bäumchen, Familien mit kleinen Kindern, bunte Läden und feine Häuser. „Sightseeing per Taxi", meinte Richard.

Für das Skizzenbuch habe ich heute noch nichts getan, aber ich bin bei der Hälfte der Seiten und guter Dinge, dass ich es nächste Woche fertigbekomme. Ich will es selbst abgeben, nicht schicken – vor allem wegen der feinen Patisserie ums Eck.

Day 42

At eight o'clock we started off towards the park with our two guests, heading for the dogs' open space. On our way we had to stop every now and then, because Lissy was panting so heavily, but everyone was in a good mood. Lissy even trotted over to some of the other dogs and took a sniff here and there. The sun was shining and many dog owners, coffee cups in hand, were chatting animatedly with friends and acquaintances. On the way home we stopped at Muse for the customary breakfast on the comfortable corner bench, underneath which Lissy also found a spot. It's warm enough to sit outside already, but the air still feels brisk.

Later on, we went to Brooklyn Bridge Park and after a nice walk, said farewell to our visitors at the ferry to Wall Street - better than taking the subway. Plus we had the chance to wave for a long time. In the taxi home I peeked out the win-

dow: blooming trees, families with small kids, colorful stores and nice houses all over the place. "Sightseeing via Taxi", as Richard called it.

Today I haven't done anything for the sketchbook yet, but I'm already halfway through, optimistic that I'll finish it by next week. I want to hand it in personally instead of sending it - especially because there's a great patisserie around the corner.

Tag 43

Heute vom Überschwemmungsalarm auf dem Handy geweckt worden und mich erinnert, dass wir gleich zu Beginn unserer Zeit hier einen Alarm aufs Handy bekamen, bei dem es um die Suche nach dem Auto eines Kindes-Entführers ging. Das war schon eine sehr spezielle Begrüßung.

Brief an meine Grundschulfreundin geschrieben, telefoniert, an einer so genannten Stakeholder-Befragung der Bundesregierung teilgenommen, bei der es um Fake News, Hass und Hetze im Netz ging, und draußen schüttete es zum Gotterbarmen. Große Bäume-Zeichnung für die Mittelseite des Skizzenbuchs gemacht und mit Paula leckeres Essen vom Vietnamesen geholt. Zu Hause konnte ich dann auch noch einen dicken Packen Post aus dem Kasten fischen: 7 Umschläge für Richard und mich!

Vorm Öffnen bewundere ich sie gerade noch und verstehe es immer weniger. Da ist eine Büchersendung dabei, die war jetzt circa 2 Monate unterwegs. Ich war schon so zornig, dass ich zu fantasieren begonnen hatte, ob es da irgendwo eine hässliche, dreckige Kiste gibt, auf der steht: „Unnütze, doofe Post für residential aliens" oder „Muss durchleuchtet, befühlt, beklopft und irgendwohin geworfen werden".

Richard ist heute zum zweiten Mal Fußball spielen mit Kolleg*innen. Das ist professionell organisiert, vom Arbeitgeber gesponsert und findet an verschiedenen Orten in Manhattan statt.

Day 43

Today I got woken up by a flood warning on my phone, which reminded me that at the very beginning of our time here we received an alarm concerning a car chase and a child kidnapper. That was quite a welcome.

Wrote a letter to my friend from elementary school, answered calls and took part in a so-called "Stakeholder Survey" by the federal government. It concerned "Fake News", hatred and harassment online. Outside it was raining hard enough to wake God's mercy. Drew a large sketch of trees in the middle of the sketchbook and got some great food from the Vietnamese place with Paula. Back at home I fished out a massive pile of mail from the box: 7 envelopes for Richard and me!

Looked at them in wonder before opening, and still didn't understand why there were so many. Among the contents is a book I have been waiting on for two months now. I'd already been so angry, that I had started to fantasize, if maybe there wasn't an ugly, dirty box somewhere, which read something like: "Useless, stupid mails for residential aliens" or "must be x-rayed, groped, knocked about, and thrown somewhere".

Richard is out playing soccer with his colleagues for the second time. It's professionally organized and takes place at different spots around Manhattan.

Tag 44

Lecker: Quiche mit Spargel und Ziegenkäse! Meine Pistazien-Croissant-Stange wartet noch. Belohnung für Hausarbeit.

Der Hundespaziergang war angenehm, aber nur weil ich meinen gerade erst gereinigten Kuschelwintermantel wieder hervorgeholt habe. Schon schade, dass uns der Frühling so vorenthalten wird dieses Jahr.

Muss mich um einen Zahnarzt-Termin kümmern. Die Praxis ist im Souterrain und sieht nicht wirklich einladend aus, aber das hilft jetzt nichts. Hatte ja insgeheim gehofft, ein wenig die Luft anhalten zu können und mich dann in Deutschland behandeln zu lassen. Aber nun ist ein Stück Füllung raus und allmählich wird's unangenehm. Wegducken hilft also nicht mehr.

Die Anmeldung zu einem Sprachkurs steht auch noch auf der Liste ... Herrje, weiß gar nicht, warum ich gerade so ein Feigling bin.

Day 44

Yummy: quiche with asparagus and goat cheese! My pistachio croissant is still pending. Reward for doing household chores.

Walking the dog felt good, but only because I took out my freshly-cleaned, cuddly winter coat again. Quite a pity that spring is being held back so long this year.

Had to take care of a dentist appointment. The doctor's office is located in a basement; and doesn't look that inviting, but that doesn't matter now. Secretly I had hoped to hold my breath a while and wait until we were in Germany again to be treated. But now a piece of the filling fell out and it's been uncomfortable. So avoiding the dentist is no longer an option.

Sign-up to a language class is still on the list too ... Oh man, I don't know, why I'm being such a coward right now.

Tag 45

Lange Metrofahrt mit einem fetten Bund bunter Tulpen im Arm – wir sind auf dem Weg zur Schwester einer Freundin aus Deutschland, die schon seit vielen Jahren in New York lebt und arbeitet. Unser erster Besuch bei Leuten, die richtig in Manhattan in einem der alten Hochhäuser wohnen. Ich bin neugierig auf alles: jemanden Neues kennenlernen und sehen, wie sie wohnen. Unsere Gastgeberin hat ihre Wohnung gekauft, als das noch für normales Geld möglich war – die einzige Möglichkeit, selbst für Menschen mit einem guten Gehalt, dableiben zu können. Manche haben noch das Glück, in Häusern mit eingefrorenen Mieten zu leben.

Wir werden sehr herzlich begrüßt, machen einen Spaziergang im nahegelegenen Teil des Central Parks und können wunderbar miteinander über die Post und Päckchen, in de-

Day 45

Had a long subway ride with a huge bunch of tulips in my arms - we are on our way to the sister of a friend from Germany, who has lived and worked here in New York for many years. It's our first visit with someone who lives in one of Upper West Side's really old blocks. I am curious about everything: meeting new people and discovering how they live. Our friend bought her flat at a time when it was available for normal money - the only opportunity, even for people with a solid wage, to be able to stay here. Some do have the luck of living in apartments with frozen rents.

We are welcomed very affectionately and start off with a walk-through a nearby part of Central Park, having great joy complaining about post and packages that are missing things, which is just as baffling to them as it is to us. Chris is a doctor and works at the local bureau of health. Pete is a musician but makes his living with other jobs.

Their flat looks exactly like what I know from movies and could be described as "typical" for the intellectual part of Manhattan. The dimensions are nice, and it is decorated with style; however, the views from the windows are rather disappointing. In Germany you would say you're looking from one tenement to the next - but here, this kind of living is still exclusive. Pete made us cherry cobbler, a typically sweet desert, which for us sadly was too sweet. Sweet is a relative concept, we already got that. But the cherry cobbler looks fantastic and we are always thankful to try something new.

nen Sachen fehlen, lästern – das ist ihr alles genauso bekannt und unverständlich wie uns. Christina ist Ärztin und arbeitet in der städtischen Gesundheitsbehörde. Ihr Partner ist Musiker, muss seinen Lebensunterhalt aber mit anderen Jobs verdienen.

Die Wohnung sieht genauso aus, wie ich sie aus Filmen kenne und als „typisch" für das intellektuelle Manhattan bezeichnen würde. Sie ist gut geschnitten und wird stilvoll bewohnt. Allerdings sind die Fensterausblicke eher enttäuschend. In Deutschland würde man sagen, man schaut von einer Mietskaserne auf die nächste – hier ist dieses Wohnen exklusiv. Peter hat uns Cherry Cobbler gemacht, etwas typisches Süßes, das uns leider wieder zu süß ist. Süß ist relativ, das haben wir schon gemerkt. Aber der Cherry Cobbler sieht wunderbar aus und wir sind immer dankbar, etwas Neues kennenzulernen.

Tag 46

Mit Annick, Emilia, Mischa und Theresa einen langen Frühlings-Spaziergang gemacht. Ich wurde gar nicht fertig damit, die blühenden Bäume in den vielen kleinen Seitenstraßen zu bewundern und zu fotografieren. Zum Brunchen ging es wieder ins „Piccoli", wir belegten eine lange Tafel, über die hinweg wir kreuz-und-quer reden und politisieren konnten.

Wir tauschen Infos aus und das gibt einem ein vertrautes Gefühl, das die Fremde sonst nicht bereithält. Wir versuchen, unser Gastland zu verstehen, und setzen gemeinsam unsere Puzzleteile zusammen. Annick bekommt über ihre Töchter viel mehr New-Yorker-Familienleben mit und das ist interessant für uns zu hören. Zum Beispiel die so genannten Play-Dates: Da sitzen die Nanny des einen Kindes und die Nanny des anderen Kindes, warten darauf, dass die Kinder ihre vereinbarte Zeit „abspielen", und dann geht es weiter zur nächsten Freizeitbeschäftigung.

Normalerweise arbeiten beide Eltern Vollzeit und die Kinder werden komplett von Nannys betreut. Die Elementary- und Middle-School – im selben Gebäude wie Paulas High-School – sind sehr beliebt. Die Eltern spenden und versuchen jahrelang im Voraus, ihre Kinder dort unterzubringen. Für die High-School wechseln sie dann aber, obwohl das Lehrkonzept die logische Fortführung des bisherigen ist. Da dort aber überwiegend Kinder aus einkommensschwachen Familien zur Schule gehen, kommt das für die wohlhabenderen Familien nicht mehr in Frage. Und ja: Wie immer geht es auch um die Hautfarbe und die kulturellen Unterschiede. Wenn ich dann von Paula höre, wie sich das immer weiter

Day 46

Had a long spring walk with Annick, Emilia, Mischa and The-resa. I couldn't stop admiring and taking pictures of all the blooming trees standing in many of the little side streets. For brunch we went at Piccoli's again, where we sat at a mas-sive table, and could chat and politicize all the way across and over.

We exchanged gossip, giving us a feeling of familiarity, we normally don't have amidst all this "strangerhood". We tried to understand our host-country, putting different pieces of the jigsaw puzzle together. Through her daughters, Annick gets to know more about New York family life, which is in-teresting for us to learn about. An example are the so-called "play-dates": that's where the nanny of the one child sits be-side the nanny of another child, waiting for them to "play

fortsetzt und die Schwarzen wiederum darüber diskutieren, wer „dark" und wer „light skin" ist, dann könnte man schon den Mut verlieren. Das gilt aber natürlich nicht!

away" the arranged time, and then it's off to the next lei-sure activity.

Normally both parents work full-time, and the children are looked after entirely by the nannies. The elementary and mid-dle school - both located in the same building as Paula's high school - are very popular. The parents donate years in ad-vance in an attempt to get their children assigned there. For high school they transfer somewhere else, even though, from an educational standpoint, it would be the logical continua-tion of what they had before. But because it's mainly attend-ed by children from lower-income families, this school is no longer considered an option for the wealthier ones. And yes: as always, it has something to do with skin color and cultur-al differences. When Paula tells me how this process contin-ues, how the black students then discuss who is "dark" and who is "light skin", it's possible to feel discouraged. But of course, that's not a choice!

Tag 47

Sitze zum ersten Mal wieder auf einer Bank im Park und kann ein bisschen schreiben. Lissy ist neben mir und muss sich wahrscheinlich erst wieder daran gewöhnen – so, jetzt hat sie sich hingelegt, sehr fein.

Seitdem ich fleißig zeichne, kommt das Schreiben zu kurz, doch es ist Endspurt fürs Skizzenbuch. Am Samstag will ich es abgeben. Werde es vermissen.

Dafür, dass ich hier jeden Tag lesen, mir neues Wissen aneignen und so viele Entdeckungen machen kann, schreiben und zeichnen, dafür bin ich echt dankbar. Geld verdienen konnte ich im Februar mal mit einem Überraschungs-Auftrag: Übersetzungen von englischen Texten ins Deutsche, inhaltlich ging es passenderweise ums Sprachenlernen und ferne Länder – perfekt.

Mittlerweile sitze ich auf einer Bank beim Spielplatz und verlängere unseren Aufenthalt mit einem Telefonat mit Nick. Es ist gerade so schön in der Sonne, und zu Hause wartet nur die lärmende Straßen-Baustelle ...

Day 47

For the first time this year I can sit on a bench in the park and write a little. Lissy is next to me and probably needs to get used to this again - now she's laid down, perfect.

Since I've been drawing diligently, the writing has been cut short a bit, but now I'm in the final stretch for the sketchbook. I plan to hand it in on Saturday. I'll miss it.

That I'm able to read, gain new knowledge, write, draw and make new experiences every day here - I'm so thankful. I even earned some money in February with a surprise job: translations of English essays into German. Content-wise, they were, appropriately, about language-learning and foreign countries - perfect.

Now I am sitting on a bench at the playground and extend our stay with a phone call with Nick. It is so nice in the sun right now, and at home there is only the noise of the construction site waiting for us...

Tag 48

Paula hat eine Auszeichnung für ihren exzellenten Notendurchschnitt bekommen! Für uns alle ein völlig neues Gefühl. Wir sind gerührt und in aufgekratzter Stimmung.

Zum zweiten Mal waren wir in Paulas Schule für die so genannte Student Led Conference, die Alternative zu einem klassischen Lehrergespräch, die unsere Schule hier als das passendere Modell für sich etabliert hat. Die Schüler*innen selbst sollen gelungene Projekte vorstellen und sagen, was sie noch verbessern wollen. Die Crew-Leader hören zu, können bei Bedarf ergänzen und die Eltern können Fragen stellen. Paulas Crew-Leader William merkte nur an, dass sich Paula ruhig trauen sollte, noch mehr vor der Klasse zu sprechen. So konnten wir uns alle mehr als zufrieden anlächeln.

Zur Belohnung ging es in ein Lokal in der Nähe – Essen im Freien! Es ist eine belebte, aber trotzdem noch gemütliche Gegend. Wir können alle und alles an uns vorbeiziehen lassen und unser Essen genießen.

Day 48

Paula received an award for her outstanding grade average today! A completely new feeling for all of us. We are touched and feeling elated.

For the second time we went to Paula's school for the so-called "Student Led Conference", an alternative to the classic conference which the school has adapted as its designated mode of parent-teacher communication. The students themselves present successful projects and talk about what they want to improve. The "crew leaders" listen to them, adding things if needed. The parents may ask questions as well. Paula's crew leader William only added that Paula should present in front of the class even more than she does now. At that we could all exchange a more-than-happy smile.

As a reward we went to a restaurant nearby - nice having lunch outside again! It is a lively, but comfortable area. We let everyone and everything pass by and enjoy our food.

Tag 49

Kirschblütenfest im „Brooklyn Botanic Garden": Nach diesem harten Winter und dem zähen Frühlingsbeginn bin ich überwältigt – mitten in den blühenden Bäumchen stehen, nach oben in den Himmel schauen und eine zarte Wolke aus weißen und rosa Blüten sehen und es schier nicht fassen können.

Obwohl großer Andrang herrscht und vor fast jedem Zweig Menschen stehen, die fotografiert werden wollen oder selbst fotografieren, bleibt für alle noch genug Zauber übrig.

Außerdem kann man an Ständen mit Holzschnitzereien, Stoffen, asiatischen Papierschirmen und vielen anderen hübschen Dingen entlang flanieren oder seinen Spaziergang in den japanischen Garten ausdehnen. Wahlweise kann man

Day 49

"Cherry blossom festival" in the Brooklyn Botanic Garden: After this harsh winter and the hardy beginning of spring I am overwhelmed - the feeling of standing in the middle of blooming trees, gazing up at the sky to see a soft cloud of white and pink blossoms, and being lost for words.

Though the crowds are big and practically every branch is occupied with someone waiting to be photographed, or taking pictures themselves, there is enough magic for everyone.

There is also the option to peruse the booths, selling wood carvings, textiles, Asian paper umbrellas and many other pretty things, or extend your walk throughout the whole park, in the Japanese gardens, for example. One can also picnic on the grass between the trees. The food matches the occasion and we enjoy it with chopsticks.

Some guests are wrapped in traditional Japanese cloth. The women are glittering in silk-robes of fantastic colors, yellow, blue, pink, beautifully embroidered, and worn with pride.

We are very impressed and looking forward to experiencing this again next year. And I bring a wooden doll home, which will always serve to remind me that spring always comes again - no matter how many blizzards the winter may send.

auch auf der Wiese zwischen den Bäumen picknicken. Das Essen passt zum Anlass und wir genießen es mit Stäbchen.

Einige Gäste sind in traditionelle japanische Gewänder gehüllt. Die Damen glitzern in Seidenroben von fantastischer Farbe, gelb, blau, rosa, wunderbar bestickt und mit Stolz getragen.

Wir sind sehr beeindruckt und freuen uns darauf, das im nächsten Jahr wieder zu erleben. Und ich trage eine Holzpuppe heim, die mich daran erinnern soll, dass es immer wieder Frühling wird – wie viele Schneestürme der Winter auch bringt.

Tag 50

Kontrastprogramm: Heute inmitten gellenden Lärms von den großen Brücken in DUMBO unterwegs, auf dem Weg zum Flohmarkt unter der Manhattan Bridge, mit Graffitis an Hausmauern, Resten von Kopfsteinpflaster, verstreuten Lädchen und Laderampen für Lagerhäuser.

Der farbenfrohe Flohmarkt wirkt bei all dem Graubraun drumherum wie eine Blumenwiese, ein Farbklecks in einer Schwarz-Weiß-Landschaft. Wir beginnen zu stöbern und versinken in anderen Zeiten. Finden riesige Garnrollen, handbemalte Glas-Dias, die Märchen für Kinder erzählen, Nägel von Eisenbahnschwellen mit Jahreszahlen, ein altes Dreirad, das so aufwendig ausgestattet ist, dass es sicher ein reiches Kind erfreut hat, Postkarten mit handkolorierten Motiven und und und – Richard und ich sind im Entdeckerfieber. Und Paula müssen wir gar nicht anstecken – sie ist von sich aus begeistert.

Day 50

Change of scenery today: out and about in DUMBO, surrounded by the shrill noise of the big bridges on our way to the flea market underneath Manhattan Bridge, accompanied by graffiti on house walls, old pieces of cobblestone, a smattering of shops, and loading ramps for the warehouses.

The colorful flea market, surrounded by all this dun, is like a flower meadow, a touch of color in a black-and-white landscape. As we browse, we dive into the past, discovering giant rolls of yarn, hand painted glass slides, telling fairy tales for children, nail-pins from railways with year markings, an old tricycle built so extraordinarily, it surely once made a rich child happy, postcards with hand colored motives, and and and - Richard and I have caught "discovery fever". And Paula does not need to be infected, she is enthusiastic all by herself.

To regain our energy we go for pizza, made in a real wood-fired oven, chicken over rice, lassi, and homemade lemonade. We're seated at the picnic tables and, because of the trains overhead, have to shout at each other for communication - but it still makes for a lot of fun.

I am looking up at the columns on the bridge and I can hardly believe, that we are actually living here - it all seems so foreign, and yet so known.

Zur Stärkung gibt es echte Holzofenpizza, Chicken over Rice, Lassi und Home Made Lemonade. Man sitzt damit an Picknicktischen und muss sich wegen des Eisenbahnlärms zur Verständigung anbrüllen, aber Spaß macht es trotzdem.

Ich blicke auf die Brückenpfeiler und kann es nicht ganz fassen, dass wir wirklich hier leben – vieles noch so fremd und doch auch schon vertraut.

Noch was

Ans Ende meiner Tagebücher schreibe ich immer: Ciao, liebes Tagebuch! Weil ich mich von einem vertrauten Notizbuch trennen muss und gleichzeitig schon auf das nächste freue.

Ob auf die „50 Tage in Brooklyn" noch einmal 50 folgen, habe ich noch nicht entschieden.

Aber wenn es wieder zurück nach Deutschland geht, werde ich noch einmal Abschied und Ankommen beschreiben. Paula wird mich daran erinnern, wenn ich loslegen soll.

Bis die Tage also!

Some more

At the end of my diaries I usually put: ciao, dear diary! Because I have to say goodbye to an entrusted diary, but at the same time look forward to the next one.

Whether the "50 days in Brooklyn" will be followed by another 50, I haven't decided yet. But it's off to Germany again I will surely describe departure and arrival once more. Paula can remind me when to start.

Until then!

Weitere Eindrücke von der neuen Heimat finden sich hier:

www.wegholz.de

In Erinnerung an Lissy

In memory of Lissy